AF469144

TRAILS OF STEAM

Volume 7 ~ Trails along the Welsh Border

by Colin Walker

Oxford Publishing Co · Oxford

SBN 86093 006 8

Printed and bound in the City of Oxford

Published by
Oxford Publishing Co.
8 The Roundway
Headington
Oxford

TRAILS ALONG THE WELSH BORDER

This book takes a look at some latter day steam haulage on the main lines following the border country separating England from Wales. Then, taking the Central Wales line, it penetrates the border for a few miles to see what a journey into the remote Welsh heartland meant for steam engines and their crews.

Throughout its length the border routes from Chester down to Shrewsbury and Newport was one of rich landscape variety with constant reminders that one was travelling the fringes of an extensive hill country. Collective or isolated heights like the Esclusham and Ruabon Mountains, the Breiddens, the Wrekin, the Caradoc range, Long Mynd and the Clee Hills all made themselves conspicuous on the run down to Hereford after which the heights of Skirrid Fawr and the Sugar Loaf announced the Black Mountains and the 'Mynydds' of South Wales.

Not surprisingly gradients abounded on some stretches like the 1 in 82½ of Gresford bank and the short, sharp climbs in both directions away from the Dee viaduct. There was that almost unbroken climb of 13 miles from the Severn valley at Shrewsbury up to the Church Stretton Gorge while beyond Hereford the taxing climbs up to the summits at Llanvihangel and Pontypool Rd. particularly from the south, with their gradients of 1 in 82 and 1 in 95, made trains hang very heavily on the drawbars of steam locomotives.

At some points where the massif approached the main lines, an attendant valley draining the uplands from the west, offered the railway an invitation, (or challenge!), to sample the delights of the Celtic interior. One such valley created by the joint efforts of the Rivers Teme and Clun provided a misleadingly passive access for the London & North Western Railway's Central Wales route to Swansea at least as far as the border market town of Knighton. What happened after that is accorded a substantial portion of this book.

On the main line routes where the interests of the London Midland and Western Regions came together the motive power was mixed. Chester was predominantly London Midland particularly on a Summer Saturday when passenger traffic to the North Wales coast was at its peak. The products from Swindon came more into their own after leaving Saltney Junction to attack the steepening grades of the climb to Gresford but in the last years of steam they never enjoyed a total monopoly. Nationalisation and subsequent regional changes brought an increasing number of London Midland and Standard engines to the line until the take-over became total.

The county town of Shrewsbury introduced the North & West main line which way back in pre-grouping times was jointly operated by both the Great Western and London & North Western companies as far as Hereford. Its mixed flavour remained a characteristic right up until the disappearance of the Western engines in 1964.

Both the North & West and Chester main lines are still graced by seasonal displays of preserved steam, of course, thanks to their reduced status as busy trunk routes but the Central Wales line now only serves as a tourist attraction and as a tenuous social and civilising link for the scattered and isolated communities of rural Wales. Its traffic is passenger only and the sequence of freight trains that daily slogged their way into the mountains are a fading memory which here receives a vivid recall.

The range of motive power over the Central Wales line was somewhat restricted but it was compensated for by the drama that surrounded steam operation in a wild and strenuous country. There were no stock performances or spectacles. Each engine made its own individual effort which light and weather further differentiated.

Any description of train working on the Central Wales line must include a special mention of the Fowler variety of the London Midland 4P 2-6-4 tank engines that headed many of the passenger trains. The service from Shrewsbury to Swansea Victoria involved a distance of some 115 miles and entailed perhaps the longest through run for a tank engine in the country over a very difficult route. The Fowler 4Ps did it with style and impressive economy.

I spent many hours on the lineside west of Knighton and enjoyed a number of trips on the single line section up to Llangunllo. After a mild start on 1 in 194 and 1 in 101 grades beside the River Teme trains soon found themselves climbing away from the river at a cruel 1 in 60 above Knucklas village where the line crossed over a 'mediaeval' castellated stone viaduct of quite exquisite character.

The climb up the Heyop Valley lasted for 3 miles, two of them at 1 in 60 followed by an easier mile at 1 in 100 to the summit tunnel near Llangunllo which boasted a quite stifling narrow bore. The passenger trains usually managed the bank single handed but for the freight trains a banker was provided at Knighton and most of them availed themselves of its services.

I had several runs on the banker and quickly discovered that my unofficial pleasures contained distinct hazards.

The problem arose because some train crews were not entirely satisfied with the amount of tractive effort provided behind the brake van and they would show their disapproval by adopting the sinister strategy of stoking up the fire on the approach to the tunnel and then opening their engine out when it entered the narrow portal.

By the time the banker entered, the smoke and fumes were at suffocation levels and desperate measures had to be taken by the banker crew (and any guests!) to cover the mouth and nostrils with a handkerchief or other suitable textile in a futile attempt to filter some air from the pungent gases.

It was a decidedly unpleasant experience and a fascinating audible memory of this dubious practice can be heard on some of Peter Handford's splendid recordings of freight trains on this climb.

Colin Walker, 1980

1652
44683

2a An Eastern Region B1 4-6-0 No 61372 working through to Llandudno rounds the curve away from the station with a Summer excursion.

CHESTER

◁ 1 A Stanier Class 5, No 44683 makes a curving departure from Chester with a Summer Saturday train for the North Wales Coast in August 1963.

◁ **2b** A vigorous exit by another Black 5, No 45188 with a Summer extra for Llandudno.

3 An unidentified 'Austerity' 2-8-0 with a down parcels train approaches the footbridge carrying the old city wall over the railway.

44916

◁ 4 Gresford Bank. Stanier Class 5 No 44916 drags a mixed freight up the gradient towards Gresford Halt.

5 In June 1962 a Western Region 'County' class 4-6-0, No 1013 *County of Dorset* chatters past Gresford Halt with the 2.40 pm from Birkenhead to Paddington.

4952

7 In the weakening light of an Autumn evening a Western Region Mogul, No 5330 passes Gresford Colliery at the top of the climb from the Dee valley with a train from Chester to Barmouth.

◁ 6 Laying a heavy pall of smoke over the station and its house a 'Hall', No 4952 *Peplow Hall* climbs wearily through Gresford Halt with a southbound freight.

8 'Hall' class No 7922 *Salford Hall* strikes off from Ruabon with the 1.12 pm express from Birkenhead to Wolverhampton.

9 In the other direction No 5942 *Doldowlod Hall* climbs the short stretch of 1 in 83 at Rhosmedre after crossing the Dee viaduct with an express from Wolverhampton to Birkenhead. ▷

5942

6964

◁ **10** 'Hall' class No 6964 *Thornbridge Hall* tops the 'hump' south of Ruabon with an up fitted freight.

11 The Dee viaduct. A Western Region 28XX 2-8-0 crosses the arches with an up freight in the hazy sun of a summer evening.

12 Chirk viaduct. A down fitted freight headed by a 'Hall' class 4-6-0 heads for Chester across the arches spanning the River Ceiriog and its water meadows. Beyond the railway viaduct can be seen the viaduct carrying the Llangollen canal.

13 Night activity at Shrewsbury. A 'Grange' No 6870 *Bodicote Grange* moves out of No 1 Bay with some empty stock. ▷

6870

14 An unkempt 'Castle' No 7011 *Banbury Castle* further disfigured by some hastily scrawled reporting numbers makes a determined climb and approaches Church Stretton with the 12.10 express from Manchester to Plymouth.

15 Another preserved 'Star', No 4079 *Pendennis Castle* climbs to Church Stretton with a preservation special. ▷

GREAT WESTERN

17 In the northbound direction a Western Mogul No 5306 between Marshbrook and Church Stretton labours up the short 1 in 112 up to the summit with a heavy train of steel. ▷

16 The 1.30 pm down fitted freight from Saltney Junction to Cardiff covers the last few yards of the climb to Church Stretton headed by 'Grange' No 6811 *Cranbourne Grange*.

5306

18 On Good Friday 1958 a 'Britannia' Pacific, No 70018 *Flying Dutchman* rushes the grade near Stokesay with the 8.45 am from Plymouth to Liverpool.

19 Ludlow. No 6873 *Caradoc Grange* coasts through Ludlow station ▷ with a relief express from Manchester to Penzance on a summer Saturday.

204

208

◁ **20** No 5038 *Morlais Castle* runs under easy steam round the Ludlow curves with Shrewsbury's classic lodging turn, the through working to Newton Abbot on the 9.5 am from Liverpool to Plymouth.

21 Following the Plymouth train was the 9.10 am Manchester-Cardiff express headed by London Midland 'Royal Scot' No 46106 *Gordon Highlander* seen here leaning to the curve through Ludlow station wearing its conspicuous non-standard smoke deflectors.

22 Approaching Ludlow from the south a Western 28XX 2-8-0 No 2892 shuffles along with a mixed freight.

23

Accelerating away from the Ludlow slack Western Region 'Hall' No 6998 *Burton Agnes Hall* nears Woofferton with an express for Plymouth. Above the engine rises the quarried eminence of Titterstone Clee Hill. ▷

5596

◁ 24 More preservation spectacles. Restored LMS 'Jubilee' class 4-6-0 No 5596 *Bahamas* approaches the south end of Dinmore tunnel with an enthusiasts special. The up and down lines separate at Dinmore and each has its own tunnel.

25 No 6000 *King George V* and No 4472 *Flying Scotsman* combine their considerable strengths as they head north from Hereford with the 'Atlantic Venturers Express'.

M
6814

◁ 26 A Western 'Grange' No 6814 *Enborne Grange* pauses at Hereford with a Sunday train to Newport.

27 Another preservation special headed this time by Gresley A4, No 4498 *Sir Nigel Gresley* takes the long curve away from Hereford on its last lap to Newport.

28 As the daylight ebbs away on an Autumn Sunday No 6918 *Sandon Hall* passes Abergavenny Junction sidings on the climb to Llanvihangel with a Swansea-Manchester express.

29 A low light shot of No 6918 before its departure from Pontypool Rd. ▷

◁ **30** Newport. A morning of hazy sunshine finds preserved 'Castle' No 4079 *Pendennis Castle* taking the west curve of Maindee Junction with a northbound special for Shrewsbury.

31 No 42390, one of the highly competent and free running London Midland 4P tanks of Fowler design sets off from Knighton on the double track section of the line to Craven Arms Junction with the 7.45 am from Swansea Victoria to Shrewsbury. On the other line the brake van of a southbound freight train can be seen waiting to enter the single line stretch up to Llangunllo with the help of the banker No 2222 which is on the right.

45283
BRITISH RAILWAYS
48706

◁ **32** Stanier Class 5 No 45283 moves off from Knighton with the 12.25 pm train from Swansea to Shrewsbury. In the goods loop an 8F No 48706 with a class H freight waits for the road up into the hills.

33 The fireman of Black 5 No 45422 which is running into Knighton with the 6.15 am from Swansea to Shrewsbury holds out the single line token from Llangunllo. The Knighton signalman collects.

34 A Western Region 22XX 0-6-0 No 2222 begins to give some rear end assistance to an 8F which is preparing to start the climb to Llangunllo with a freight for Llandilo.

35 Class 5, No 45143 gathers as much speed as it can on the gently rising gradient up the Teme valley out of Knighton before the heavy work begins. The train is the 12 noon from Shrewsbury to Swansea. ▷

36 Two 8Fs Nos 48761 and 48706 begin to feel the 1 in 60 as they approach Knucklas with the 9.45 am freight from Stafford to Swansea.

37 No 48732 makes a fine effort as it nears Knucklas Halt with the ▷ 5.55 am freight from Shrewsbury to Swansea.

48732

38 As heavy rain sets in No 48737 is opened up strongly ready to climb round the curve at Knucklas with the 9.45 am from Stafford to Pontadulais.

39 The banker No 48478 gives some vigorous support at the brake van end. Knucklas viaduct can be seen beyond the station nameboard. ▷

KNUCKL
HALT

40 Class 5 No 44835 passes Knucklas Halt with a southbound freight.

41 A photograph from the platform end at Knucklas Halt shows ▷ No 44835 obscured by steam from its massive effort on the worst part of the exposed embanked curve leading onto the viaduct. 8F No 48478 is the banker.

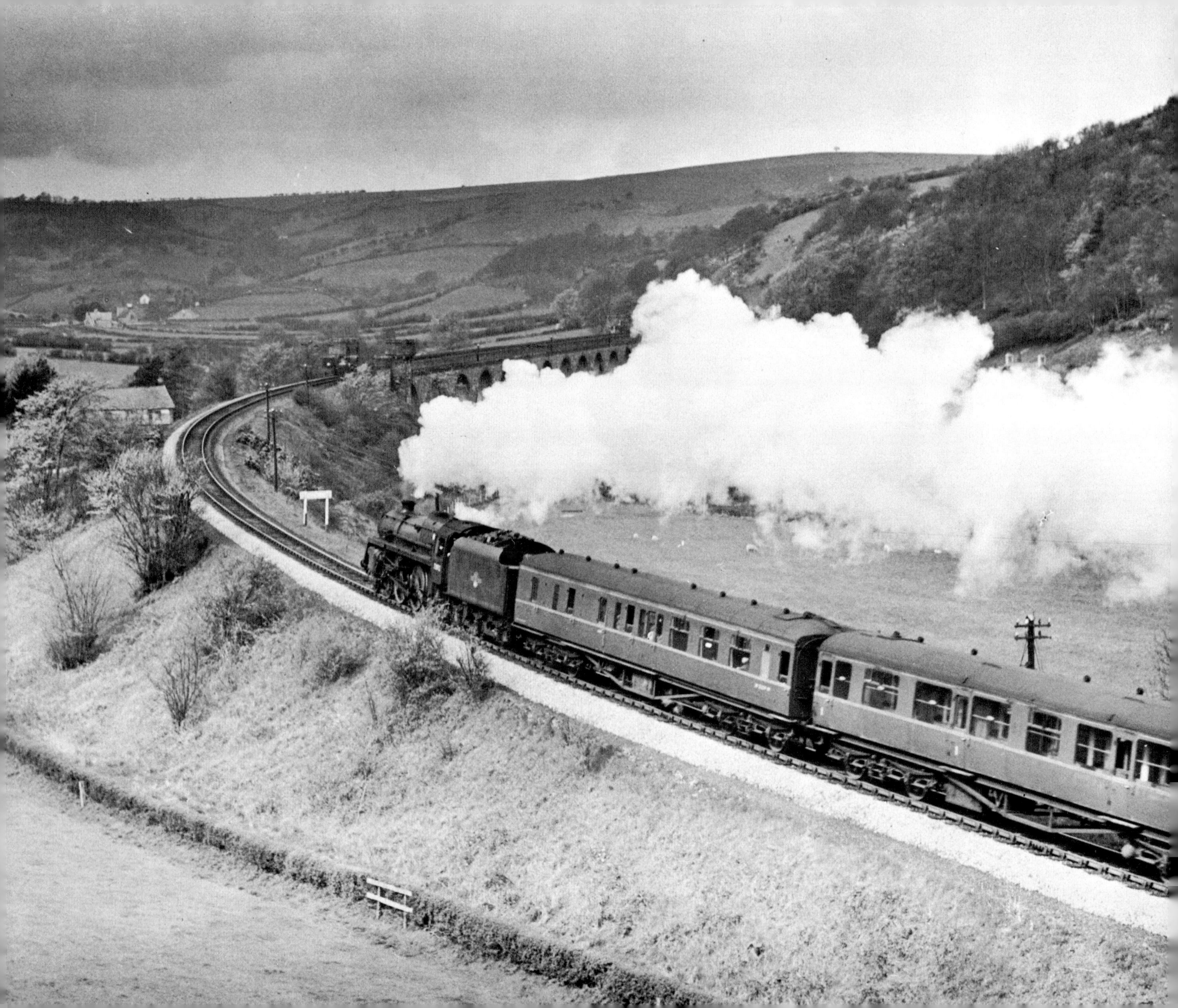

◁ **42** From the hillside on the other side of the line a Standard Class 5 No 73092 is seen climbing towards the viaduct with the 12 noon train from Shrewsbury to Swansea Victoria.

43 Coasting down the bank is Fowler 4P tank No 42305 with the 6.15 am from Swansea to Shrewsbury.

44 A maximum effort by Class 5 No 45190 blasting its way towards the viaduct with the 9.10 am class D freight from Shrewsbury to Llandilo.

▷

45 At the back of the train the driver of the banker, No 48478 snatches a look back at the camera as he crosses the arches.

45422

◁ **46** A fine unassisted effort by Class 5 No 45422 heading the 9.10 am Shrewsbury-Llandilo freight.

47 The railway through Knucklas runs east-west. This shot from Castle Hill on the north side of the viaduct shows No 48478 banking an afternoon freight.

48 In drenching rain a Standard 5 No 73026 climbs away from the viaduct with the 9.10 am class D freight from Shrewsbury to Llandilo Junction.

49 Running under Class A headlamps Fowler Class 4P tank No 42387 climbs comfortably up the 1 in 60 with an afternoon train from Shrewsbury to Swansea.

50 In a rock cutting beyond Knucklas 8F No 48328 makes a forbidding picture as it toils up the grade with an evening class H goods train.

51 At the end of the train ▷ Western 0-6-0 No 2222 provides a spirited push.

52 *Across next double page* The south side of the viaduct shows Class 5 No 44835 crossing with the 12 noon train from Shrewsbury to Swansea Victoria.

20 T
246693

48307

◁ **53** On the way up the Heyop valley No 48307 drags the 9.45 am freight from Stafford to Pontadulais towards the summit tunnel.

54 Yet another 8F No 48110 gains height up the Heyop valley with a freight for Llandilo.

45283

◁ **55** Half way up. No 45283 makes light work of the 3 coach 2.50 pm from Shrewsbury to Swansea.

56 Towards the end of the day a Fowler 4P tank No 42307 approaches the summit tunnel on the 1 in 100 with the 5.45 pm train from Shrewsbury to Swansea.

57 Driver Stan Ayres from Shrewsbury shed blows the brake off his engine 8F No 48760 before setting off from Llangunllo with a freight for Shrewsbury.

58 The Knighton banker No 2222 is coupled onto 8F No 48760 for the return journey from Llangunllo. The two are here seen about to enter Llangunllo tunnel with a freight from Swansea to Shrewsbury. ▷

59 The Knighton banker No 48478 provides another double headed descent from Llangunllo for the 8.25 am from Swansea East Dock to Crewe which is being hauled by No 48768.